Those Rebels, John & Tom

BY

BARBARA KERLEY

ILLUSTRATED BY

EDWIN FOTHERINGHAM

SCHOLASTIC PRESS ★ NEW YORK

THE TRUE STORY OF HOW

ONE GENTLEMAN—SHORT AND STOUT—

AND ANOTHER—TALL AND LEAN—

FORMED A SURPRISING ALLIANCE,

COMMITTED TREASON,

AND HELPED LAUNCH A NEW NATION.

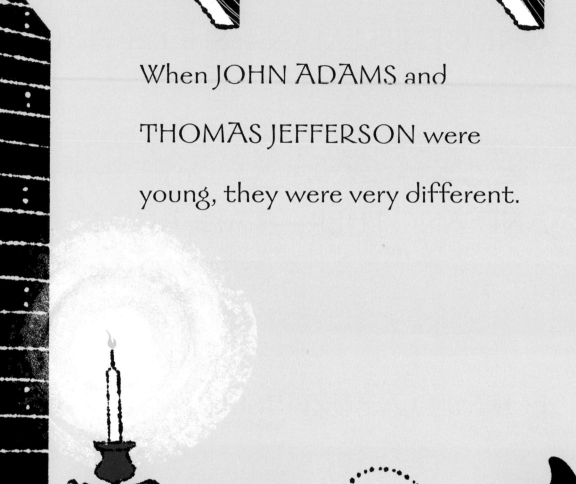

When JOHN ADAMS and

THOMAS JEFFERSON were

young, they were very different.

JOHN skipped school to fly kites and shoot marbles. He loved swimming, hunting, wrestling—and the occasional boxing match, just for kicks.

TOM didn't skip school.

He skipped recess—to study Greek grammar.

He loved dancing, playing the violin, and reading

all the books in his father's library.

When JOHN and TOM
grew up, they were even *more* different.
JOHN liked to talk. And talk. In college,
he joined a debating club so that he could talk
some more. And when he became a lawyer, he
found he could talk for hours without using any
notes—a handy skill in the courtroom.
He loved nothing more than to battle
wits in a lively argument.

TOM was shy, and dreaded speaking in front of
crowds. Talking too loudly made his voice hoarse. When
he became a lawyer, he found he didn't enjoy presenting
cases to the jury—a bit of a problem in the courtroom.
He hated arguments. If he had an idea,
he quietly wrote it down.

JOHN lived in a sturdy farmhouse in Braintree, Massachusetts. He found farming "very muddy," but he liked it "very well"—clearing stumps to plow his fields and then carting out manure to fertilize them.

When he wasn't in the courtroom, he planted corn, pruned fruit trees, and chased his chickens and ducks.

TOM leveled a mountain to build his estate of Monticello in Virginia. Architecture was one of his "favorite amusements"—calculating windows, walls, and wainscots to a sixteenth of an inch.

When he wasn't in the courtroom, he maintained his accounts, surveyed his lands, and dined on chicken and duck.

Monticello

JOHN and TOM were indeed very different, but they did have two things in common: They both cared deeply about the American colonies, and neither of them cared much for George.

George lived across the ocean in England, in a grand and glorious palace. He was the latest in a long line of kings who had ruled colonists in America.

Some people called him "Good King George."

JOHN and TOM called him a TYRANT.

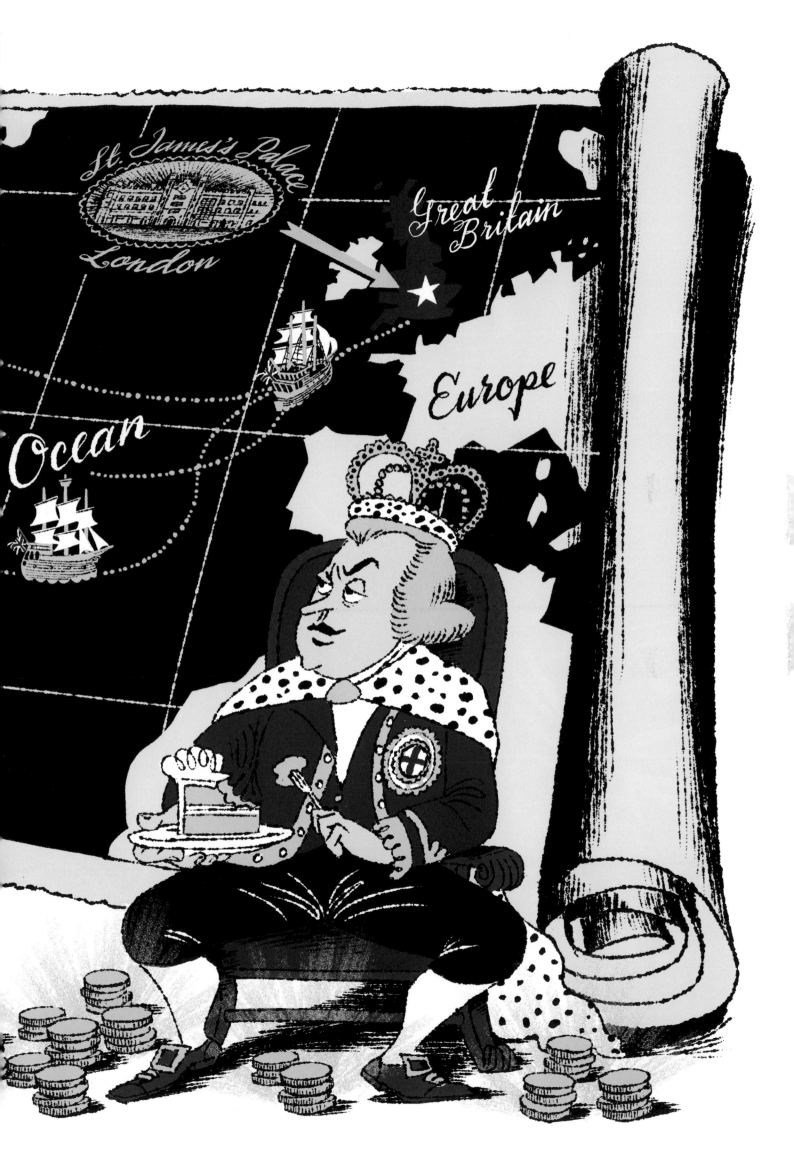

George and his government took away Americans' right to a fair trial. They shut down public meetings. George's army occupied the city of Boston, and his navy patrolled the Atlantic Ocean from England clear to the Virginia coast.

When JOHN stayed in Boston for work, George's troops exercised early each morning—fifes squealing, feet stomping, and drums rat-a-tat-tatting. How was anyone supposed to sleep through a racket like *that*?

When TOM sent his tobacco downriver to market, he could sell it to no country but England, whatever the price. How could anyone pay the bills with a racket like *that*?

And then there were all those taxes! A tax on sugar. On coffee and tea.
On glass, on paint, and on calico cloth. Newspapers, contracts, even decks of cards!
King George and his government taxed them all. They thought America was nothing
but a big fat piggy bank to be turned upside down and shaken for coins.

And so, in the fall of 1774, a group of Americans planned a meeting in
Philadelphia—a Continental Congress—to figure out what to do about it.
SOMETHING HAD TO CHANGE!

JOHN kissed his family good-bye and proudly accepted a spot with the Massachusetts delegation. When he reached Philadelphia, he was struck by the neatly laid-out streets and the elegant buildings. And oh, the food!

But when he met his fellow delegates, he fretted: Each man had his own "character and temper," his own "principles and views." Somehow these "fifty gentlemen, total strangers," would need to join forces.

JOHN thought the fledgling congress "a nursery of American statesmen." Could he and the other delegates learn how to unite the separate colonies in one common purpose?

Day after day, the delegates met to discuss their problems with George. "Tedious indeed is our business—SLOW AS SNAILS," JOHN wrote home to his wife, Abigail.

Choosing a course of action would not be easy.

In the summer of 1775, TOM kissed his family good-bye and proudly rode into Philadelphia to join the Virginia delegation. He toured the museums and drank punch in the taverns. And oh, the shopping!

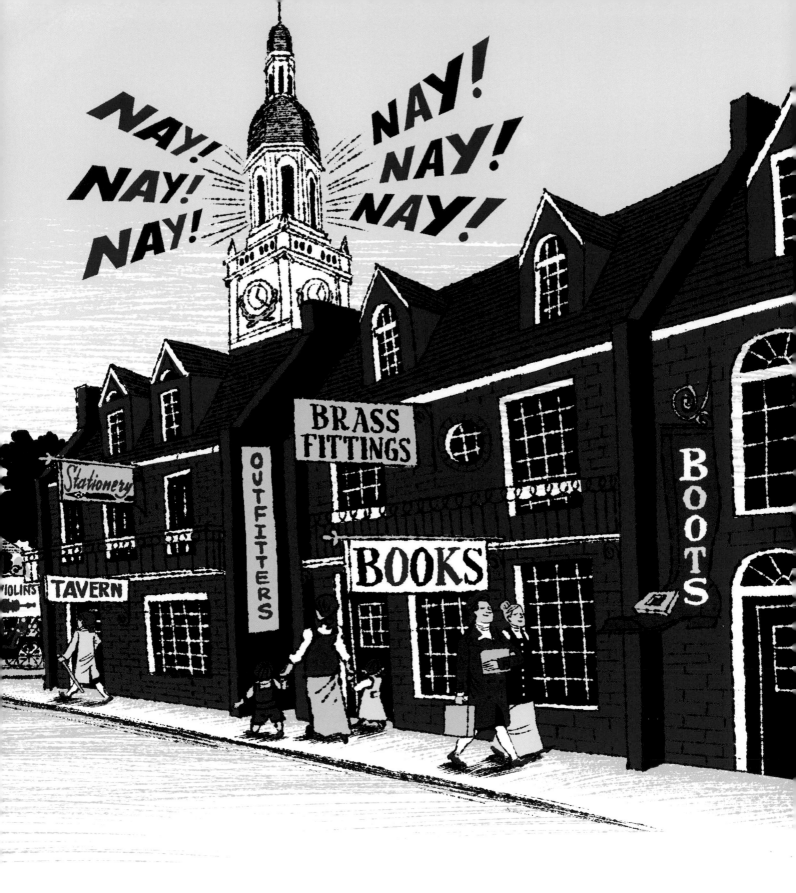

He arrived already famous for a pamphlet he'd written calling King George "a blot on the page of history." But as TOM took his seat in Congress, he quickly grew appalled: The delegates agreed on so little, and argued so much! Would they ever reach a consensus on what to do? And how could TOM possibly make himself heard above all that noise?

As he took stock of the new delegate from Virginia, JOHN—the son of a farmer and shoemaker from the North—couldn't help noticing that TOM was impeccably dressed and very soft-spoken, with gracious manners that pleased everyone.

He was also quite tall.

And TOM—the son of an aristocratic planter from the South—couldn't help noticing that JOHN was plainly dressed and spoke rather bluntly, with gruff manners that sometimes pleased almost no one.

He was also rather short.

TOM watched astounded as John battled hour after hour through heated debate, tapping the floor with his walking stick to hammer the words home. How could anyone love to argue that much?

And JOHN noted with astonishment that in Congress, TOM slumped down in his chair and never "uttered three sentences together." How could anyone who cared that much about America sit silently by?

Congress had just established a Continental
army to fight for colonists' rights. And
TOM had brought to Philadelphia a
powerful weapon of his own: a pen,
and the skill to use it better than
almost any man in America.
The delegates now turned to TOM
and his mighty pen to justify why
Americans were taking up arms.

He lunged, parried,

and skewered the

policies of King

George and his

government.

TOM might be silent in Congress, JOHN realized, but he wasn't afraid to answer King George with his pen. In fact, Tom was "so prompt, frank, explicit, and decisive" in private conversation that he soon "seized upon" John's heart.

And John's constant arguing might annoy many of those in Congress, but underneath the bluster, Tom discovered, was a man "so amiable," he later wrote a friend, "that I pronounce you will love him if ever you become acquainted with him."

The two very different men sensed

that, working together, they

might accomplish more than

by working alone. Perhaps

they could compel

their fellow delegates

to action.

Endless debate, they knew, was no longer an option.

King George's troops had already shot colonists in Lexington and Concord and burned Charlestown to the ground. George now vowed "to put a speedy end" to the "rebellion" in the colonies—and punish the rebels for treason.

By 1776, JOHN and TOM felt the time had come for America to break from King George and declare independence.

But many delegates still had doubts.

How could a small gathering

of colonies square off

against perhaps the

MIGHTIEST

COUNTRY IN

THE WORLD?

America

Great Britain

France

Spain

Atlantic Ocean

Africa

JOHN and TOM knew that a united America depended on a unanimous vote. Could John's powers of persuasion and Tom's skill with a pen convince the naysayers to vote yea?

If so, Congress would need to prepare a statement to the world, explaining why America should be free. Who could write such a document?

More than any other delegate in Congress, John had championed the cause of independence. "You should do it," Tom told him.

NAY!

YEA!

"Oh! No," John exclaimed. Any declaration *he* wrote would be severely criticized, for some delegates, he conceded, found him "obnoxious." The declaration should be written by a delegate from Virginia—the oldest and most powerful colony in America. More importantly, John told Tom, "You can write ten times better than I can."

"Well," Tom replied, "if you are decided, I will do as well as I can."

YEA!
NAY!

In the quiet of his rooms on Market Street, TOM worked on the Declaration of Independence, trying to craft "an expression of the American mind" in terms "so plain and firm" that people around the world would rally to America's side. He began with a statement of basic freedoms and ended with a long list of grievances against King George. One grievance Tom included was slavery—an issue he had struggled with for years. It was a "cruel" institution, Tom wrote, and George thwarted every attempt America made to prohibit it.

And yet, like many men in Congress, Tom himself owned slaves. As he penned this document on freedom, his fourteen-year-old slave, Bob Hemings, brought him tea.

Hour after hour, Tom sat at his little desk, writing and thinking and writing some more.

Meanwhile, JOHN
prepared himself for "the greatest debate
of all"—the vote on independence.

Storm clouds gathered as he stood and faced Congress. Above the crack
of lightning and the boom of thunder, John spoke on, trying to convince the
last naysayers to change their minds.

From his place with the Virginia delegation, TOM marveled as John
rallied the delegates. His "power of thought and expression," Tom later
wrote, "moved us from our seats."

Finally, the next morning, after almost two years of turmoil, a united America was ready to vote YEA!

The delegates now turned to Tom's declaration. He squirmed and suffered as they fine-tuned phrases and trimmed passages, including his condemnation of slavery—an issue the country would not resolve for almost one hundred years.

They cut and cut until soon Tom's work was only one page long: an expression, in terms plain and firm, of American independence.

We . . . solemnly publish and declare, That these

United Colonies are, and of Right ought to be Free and

Independent States; that they are Absolved from all

Allegiance to the British Crown. . . . And for the support

of this Declaration, . . . we mutually pledge to each

other our Lives, our Fortunes and our sacred Honor.

In cities and towns, bells rang out
as the declaration was read aloud.
Americans paraded, lit bonfires,
and toasted farewell to England.
In New York City, they even
pulled down the statue
of Good King George!
Throughout the states—
the *united* states—Americans
celebrated the end of
British oppression.

They savored the promise of a new future.
And they cheered the group of men who left
behind family and friends to meet in Philadelphia:

Hancock, Lee, Sherman, Livingston,

Franklin, Rush, Rodney, Harrison,

and all the others who launched

a new nation . . .

our sacred Honor.

John Hancock

Francis Lightfoot Lee

Roger Sherman   Step. Hopkins

Phil. Livingston   Samuel Chase

Edward Rutledge j.   Benjamin Rush

Benj. Franklin   Josiah Bartlett

                        Cæsar Rodney

John Penn

Benj Harrison   Lyman Hall

                        John Adams

Jno Witherspoon

Th Jefferson

... with THOSE REBELS, JOHN and TOM.

For fifteen years after the Declaration of Independence was signed, John and Tom remained friends.

From 1784 until 1788, both men lived in Europe as representatives for the newly formed United States of America. John and Tom spent many pleasant hours together—first in Auteuil, France, and later in London, England—deepening their friendship even further.

Still, they had their differences. One was their attitude toward slavery. The institution was "hateful," John declared, and he was proud never to have owned a slave. Tom, however, owned many slaves—in 1776, close to two hundred. In this he was not alone. At least a third of the delegates to the Continental Congress were or had been slaveholders, including John Hancock, Benjamin Franklin, and George Washington, America's first president. Tom wrote about the evils of slavery, but freed only a handful of his own slaves during his lifetime.

Another difference between John and Tom was their contrasting view about what shape the American government should take, especially after they returned home from Europe. During George Washington's presidency, through John's, and on into Tom's, John and Tom found themselves on different sides of a nationwide debate: How strong should the power of the president be? How much influence should Congress and the Supreme Court have? And how much control should remain with state governments?

John aligned himself with those who believed that a powerful central government was essential to unite the country. To him, this central government represented the unity that the colonies had forged in order to achieve independence. In that unity, he thought, was the strength necessary to best secure the future of the country.

Tom, on the other hand, was a supporter of states' rights. In his eyes, creating too strong a central government would be akin to setting up a new king, when the whole point of declaring independence had been to *free* America from a tyrannical king. Too powerful a central government, Tom thought, would hinder personal rights and freedoms.

John and Tom each felt the other to have lost sight of what they had worked so hard to achieve in 1776. The debate grew fiercer, the politics more ugly, until ultimately, they did not speak or write to each other for eleven years.

Then a mutual friend tried to patch things up, urging John to write to Tom. And so, on January 1, 1812, John wrote a short note wishing Tom a happy new year.

Tom wrote back, warmly recalling when, "beset with difficulties and dangers," they were "fellow laborers" in the struggle for independence.

Soon John and Tom were corresponding regularly. "You and I ought not to die, before We have explained ourselves to each other," John wrote, and Tom agreed. They made peace with their differences and wrote of books, politics, and their families.

They also reflected on the long passage of years and looked together toward the future. "I think with you that it is a good world on the whole," Tom wrote. "I steer my bark with Hope in the head, leaving Fear astern."

"I admire your Navigation and should like to sail with you," John replied. And though old age had robbed him of his strength, he assured Tom, "While I breathe I shall be your friend."

By the beginning of July 1826, John, now ninety years old, and Tom, now eighty-three, were both very ill. On July 3, Tom, in his sickbed at Monticello, awoke from a coma, thinking it the Fourth. His family replied that it would be soon. Almost five hundred miles away, in Braintree, John also drifted in and out of consciousness.

John and Tom both lived through the night, dying just a few hours apart on July 4, 1826 —America's fiftieth birthday. When told it was the Fourth, John had replied, "It is a great day. It is a *good* day."

A facsimile of the Declaration of Independence.
Here you can see all the signatures as they appear on the original document.

QUOTATIONS IN THE TEXT ARE DRAWN FROM THE FOLLOWING SOURCES:

"very muddy" and "very well": L. H. Butterfield, ed., *Diary and Autobiography of John Adams* (Cambridge, MA: Belknap Press of Harvard University Press, 1961), 3:258.

"favorite amusements": *Thomas Jefferson Encyclopedia*, s.v. "Architecture is my delight . . . (Quotation)," http://www.monticello.org/site/jefferson/architecture-my-delightquotation.

"Good King George": appears in numerous books and magazines, including *Blackwood's Edinburgh Magazine, Harper's New Monthly Magazine,* and the *Gentleman's Magazine.*

"character and temper", "principles and views", and "fifty gentlemen . . .": Charles Francis Adams, ed., *Familiar Letters of John Adams and His Wife Abigail Adams, During the Revolution* (Boston: Houghton Mifflin, 1875), 44.

"a nursery . . .": Robert J. Taylor, Mary-Jo Kline, and Gregg L. Lint, eds., *Papers of John Adams* (Cambridge, MA: Belknap Press of Harvard University Press, 1977), 2:99.

"Tedious indeed . . .": Adams, *Familiar Letters,* 42.

"a blot . . .": Adrienne Koch and William Peden, eds., *The Life and Selected Writings of Thomas Jefferson* (New York: Modern Library / Random House, 1944), 310.

"uttered three . . .": Charles Francis Adams, ed., *The Works of John Adams, Second President of the United States* (Boston: Charles C. Little and James Brown, 1850), 2:511.

"so prompt . . ." and "seized upon": Adams, *Works of John Adams,* 2:514.

"so amiable . . .": *Thomas Jefferson Encyclopedia*, s.v. "John Adams," http://www.monticello.org/site/jefferson/john-adams.

"to put a speedy end" and "rebellion": "His Majesty's Most Gracious Speech to Both Houses of Parliament, on Friday, October 27, 1775," http://memory.loc.gov/cgi-bin/query/r?ammem/rbpe:@field(DOCID+@lit(rbpe1440150a)).

"You should . . .", "Oh! No", "obnoxious", "You can . . .", and "Well, if you . . .": Adams, *Works of John Adams,* 2:514.

"an expression . . ." and "so plain . . .": H. A. Washington, ed., *The Writings of Thomas Jefferson* (New York: H. W. Derby, 1861), 7:407.

"cruel": Declaration of Independence, Jefferson's rough draft, http://www.ushistory.org/declaration/document/rough.htm.

"the greatest . . .": David McCullough, *John Adams* (New York: Simon and Schuster, 2001), 125.

"power of . . .": McCullough, *John Adams,* 127.

"We . . . solemnly . . .": Declaration of Independence, http://www.archives.gov/exhibits/charters/declaration_transcript.html.

QUOTATIONS IN THE AUTHOR'S NOTE ARE DRAWN FROM THE FOLLOWING SOURCES:

"hateful": Charles Francis Adams, ed., *The Works of John Adams, Second President of the United States* (Boston: Little, Brown, 1854), 9:93.

"beset with . . ." and "fellow laborers": Lester J. Cappon, ed., *The Adams-Jefferson Letters: The Complete Correspondence Between Thomas Jefferson and Abigail and John Adams* (Chapel Hill: University of North Carolina Press, 1959), 2:291.

"You and I . . .": Cappon, *Adams-Jefferson Letters,* 2:358.

"I think with you . . ." and "I steer my bark . . .": Cappon, *Adams-Jefferson Letters,* 2:467.

"I admire your . . .": Cappon, *Adams-Jefferson Letters,* 2:471.

"While I breathe . . .": Cappon, *Adams-Jefferson Letters,* 2:610.

"It is a great . . .": McCullough, *John Adams,* 646.

Special thanks to Dr. Jason Matthew Opal, associate professor of history, McGill University, for fact-checking the book.

Image of the Declaration of Independence 8893419 © DNY59 provided by Istock.

For my dad, who first introduced me to John and Tom—BK

For Becky, Anna, and Joe, with love—EF

Text copyright © 2012 by Barbara Kerley ★ Illustrations copyright © 2012 by Edwin Fotheringham ★ All rights reserved. Published by Scholastic Press, an imprint of Scholastic Inc., *Publishers since 1920.* SCHOLASTIC, SCHOLASTIC PRESS, and associated logos are trademarks and/or registered trademarks of Scholastic Inc. ★ No part of this publication may be reproduced, stored in a retrieval system, or transmitted in any form or by any means, electronic, mechanical, photocopying, recording, or otherwise, without written permission of the publisher. For information regarding permission, write to Scholastic Inc., Attention: Permissions Department, 557 Broadway, New York, NY 10012. ★ LIBRARY OF CONGRESS CATALOGING-IN-PUBLICATION DATA ★ Kerley, Barbara. Those rebels, John and Tom / by Barbara Kerley ; illustrated by Edwin Fotheringham. p. cm. Includes bibliographical references and index. ★ ISBN 978-0-545-22268-6 (alk. paper) ★ 1. Adams, John, 1735-1826—Juvenile literature. 2. Jefferson, Thomas, 1743-1826—Juvenile literature. 3. United States. Declaration of Independence—Signers—Juvenile literature. I. Fotheringham, Edwin, ill. II. Title. ★ E221.K47 2012   973.4'40922—dc222011002131 ★ 10 9 8 7 6 5 4 3 2 1   12 13 14 15 16 ★ Printed in Singapore 46 ★ First edition, January 2012 ★ The text type was set in Galahad. The display type was set in Clarendon Bold and P22 Parrish Roman. The illustrations were done in digital media. Art direction and book design by Marijka Kostiw

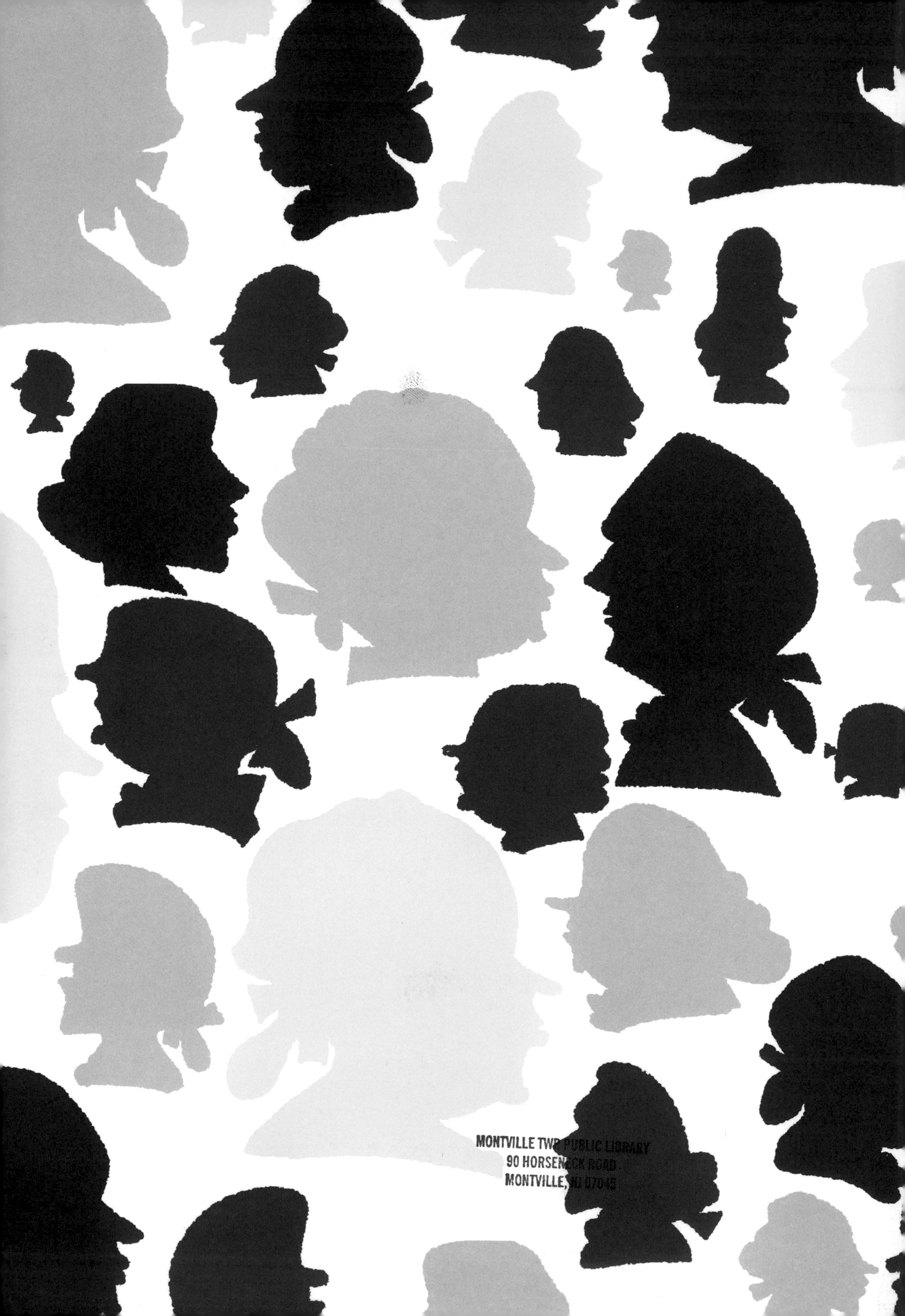